A SALES MANAGER'S
ROAD MAP
TO DYNAMIC SALES PERFORMANCE

24 Powerful Tips & Stories to Build
A Highly Productive Sales Force

Charlie Hauck   Fred Liesong

Copyright © 2016, Growth Dynamics.
All rights reserved.

No part of this book may be reproduced or transmitted in any form or by any means, electronic or mechanical, including photocopying, recording, or by any information retrieval system, without permission in writing from the publisher.

Writing & Publishing Process by PlugAndPlayPublishing.com
Book Cover by Tracey Miller | TraceOfStyle.com
Edited by Jenny Butterfield & E. D. Sewell
Photography by E. D. Sewell | EdSewell.com

ISBN: 1539028488
EAN-13: 978-1539028482

Disclaimer: This book contains opinions, ideas, experiences, and exercises. The purchaser and/or reader of these materials assumes all responsibility for the use of this information. Authors, Growth Dynamics, LLC, and Publisher assume no responsibility and/or liability whatsoever for any purchaser and/or reader of these materials.

Dedication

This book salutes the Sales Managers who face the everyday challenges of leading and directing the diverse sales teams that Growth Dynamics has worked with for nearly 20 years. We feel this group of managers deserves as much of the credit for the successes those sales teams have generated as anyone, as they are often left to figure it out under live fire without much more than a strong will and relentless pursuit of success.

A great deal of time and effort in a sales manager's existence is spent after the lights are off, the offices are closed, and there's no one else around to bounce ideas off of or share a theory about how to win even more of the market. Both of us, the principals at Growth Dynamics, have lived in that arena and know the energy and commitment it takes to manage well. So that's why we dedicate this book to a group of people in the office that are often overlooked when the dust settles and the results are positive but are frequently in the cross hairs when goals or quotas aren't hit.

We have spent many hours with managers of all stripes, listening to their stories and concerns about business up and downs and the seesaw of being perceived as either too soft by upper management or too harsh by the people they lead. It takes a unique sense of balance to satisfy all the people they serve, from customers wanting their attention when a sales person won't cut a price, sales people wanting their understanding when a quarter is going badly, and upper management wanting them to produce no matter what the circumstances.

So this book is for those Sales Managers that are always on the job, sometimes as the owners of agencies, often as the best sales people on the team, the epitome of the title "player-coach" and the ones that are also the HR department on top of everything else they do. We know you are out there, and we want you know that we wrote this for all of you.

Table Of Contents

Read This First 1

SECTION 1: Mindset 7

Call Me KOWISO, Because I Know One When 11
I See One!

I Love That Guy's Work, But I Just Don't Like 15
Him

My People Love Me, So Why Won't They Sell 17
For Me?

Is Honesty Always The Best Policy? 19

Should You Really Have An Open Door Policy? 21
Being Available Isn't Always Good.

Have You Made Enough Deposits To Cover That 23
Withdrawal?

Don't Let Climbing The Ladder Make You Less 25
Aware

The Power of Punctuation 27

SECTION 2: Activity 29

If You Don't Inspect It, You Can't Expect It 33

The Pipeline Is Full, But The Results Are Lacking............. 35

Delegation: Problem Solver or Nightmare Creator? 37

How Long Does It Take To Change The Numbers?.......... 39

Are All These Meetings Really Necessary? 41

The Worst Time To Dig A Well Is When You Are 45
Thirsty

The Right Language Helps Hit Goals 47

Who's Problem Is It Anyway? 49

SECTION 3: Process 51

Moving Your Team Up The Level Of Effort Ladder 55

Evaluations: Why Isn't Once A Year Enough? 59

Why Do I Have To Tell Everyone Three Times What 61
I Want Done?

Motivation: Isn't That Part Of My Job? 63

Everyone Loves A Year-End Bonus, Don't They? 65

Leading, Managing, Or Administrating, Pick One 67

Your Job Isn't Finished When Someone Accepts Your 71
Job Offer

Must All Salespeople Follow The Same Rules? 73

Final Thoughts 77

About Charlie Hauck 79

About Fred Liesong 81

About Growth Dynamics 83

Read This First

This book is for Manufacturers Reps, Manufacturers, Wholesalers, Distributors and Contractors, but mostly, it is written for the people that manage those businesses.

Don't be fooled though, as this book isn't going to connect with everyone that is in the above list. With that being said, we want to give you an opportunity to put this book right back down and not read another page. If you are looking for a book about the warm and fuzzy part of managing people, you are not going to find it in the pages that follow.

So consider this message a fair warning that you are not about to read a lot of feel-good stories about how great it is to be a leader or how wonderful it is to be a manager in the world of sales.

Managing People Is Hard.

That is, managing at the highest levels of professionalism is hard. And, in many cases, this high level of professionalism is considerably more difficult than most managers ever believed it could be when they transitioned from producer to manager.

The challenge that many managers/leaders never fully face is that managing is much more than just being a "people person" (whatever that might mean) and having a history of being the highest producing salesperson. There is no doubt that some people are more gifted at managing than others. But those who are so gifted that they don't have to work at mastering the skills, learning new approaches, and refining those gifts are few and far between.

There is no ivory tower theory anywhere in these pages. This book captures the real world experiences that our clients have shared with us over the years. What you are about to read is not a bunch of theory, but tried and proven tactics and strategies that work where the rubber meets the road.

The clients who spoke with us ended up daring themselves to try something different or daring themselves to challenge their perception of what was really taking place when a manager and his or her team have to work together and consistently produce results.

We do not expect anyone to need all the lessons in this book, but we hope every reader will relate to a few of the scenarios or situations that frustrate them the most or leave them wondering why things did not work out as they expected.

For your convenience, we've broken this book into three sections that make up our MAP: MINDSET, ACTIVITY, and PROCESS. Being proficient at each of these components is critical for sustained sales success.

Each section contains eight chapters. Each chapter begins with a summary, so you can quickly glance at each one and decide how it applies to your world. After each summary, we move into stories about how a client overcame the challenge and how you can too.

No matter where you sit in a management team, or how much experience you've accumulated in your career, we believe that the insights on each of these pages may provide you with enough of a different approach to merit the little bit of time it would take to read it from cover to cover.

Beyond that, we think this book might be a good resource, a place for you to search for answers when a whole team or an individual seems more intent on pushing your buttons or proving a point rather than really doing their jobs.

Over the years, we've had the benefit of working with leaders and managers in all sorts of teams and organizations, and that experience has taught us this simple truth: When the student is ready, the teacher will appear. So please give yourself the chance to let that come true for you, and keep this little volume close by as you pursue your passion of becoming a truly effective leader.

One more thing before you dive in looking for a magic bullet: Over the years, the people who have proven to be our best students have always tended to be the ones that paid more than lip service to the phrase "room for improvement." They knew that growing was about professional development and not about them as people. In other words, their willingness to set aside ego driven personal emotions allowed them to become both coachable and trainable on the professional level.

What happened over the course of our time working with these folks is that they realized that to grow both personally and professionally, what they were doing yesterday wasn't necessarily going to be the most productive or profitable strategy for tomorrow.

So, the choice is yours on whether or not you take this first step in following the lead of those who developed an open mindset.

Whether you are the top-dog in a rep agency, in charge of the sales team, or perhaps doing both, what you are about to read will provide an opportunity to improve your team's performance and to experience more satisfaction, both personally and professionally.

Here's to a future of potential reached and personal satisfaction!

Charlie Hauck & Fred Liesong

"Just as Charlie and Fred clarified some of the challenges of selling more effectively, they have made managing our sales team more consistent and less stressful. These guys share some concepts any manager can benefit from reading and applying."

Eric Lewis, President
Mullen Incorporated | St. Petersburg, FL

"As a manufacturer, I work with lots of agencies, and the ones that work on managing their people are the agencies that consistently produce the best results. Liesong and Hauck have the information and ideas that make the difference between teams that are OK and teams that are industry leaders. Give your team a boost by taking some advice from these guys."

Marc Palasini, National Sales Manager
Plumbing and Irrigation
North American Pipe Corporation | Janesville, WI

"Growth Dynamics proves once again they get what makes sales teams successful. This information works because it keeps the message consistent and instantly useful in a manager's world."

Michelle Lewnes-Dadas, VP
Preferred Sales Inc. | Hermitage, PA

"Growth Dynamics proves once again they get what makes sales teams successful. This information works because it keeps the message consistent and instantly useful in a manager's world."

Alan Tingler, CEO
Smith and Stevenson | Charlotte, NC

SECTION 1
Mindset

Hauck & Liesong

SECTION 1
Mindset

Whether you believe you can or cannot, you are right. If you watch or listen closely enough, you can observe this old adage being validated every day. But what does this have to do with being a successful manager or leader? The connection might be more important than you first realize as you strive to become the type of leader people want to follow and go to work for every day.

Which should come first, the mindset of success or success itself? For those that want to wait to be successful before thinking like you already are, the wait can often seem like an eternity. The winners are the professionals who understand that they must think the way a successful person would think and act the way a successful person would act before they can become successful. Whether you believe you can or cannot, you are definitely right!

The most successful managers develop the right beliefs and courage to support mastering the skills required to lead the teams that will rely on them. It is just as important to learn how to manage the internal messaging to create a positive outcome as it is to learn how to read spreadsheets, sales records, and business plans. If the courage to accept the challenges of managing others is not present, the tools and tactics will not save the day. If your beliefs say that people will always just do things the way they choose to do them, why would you even attempt to learn how to influence them?

This chapter provides you with real world lessons on why "how you think" about success in a management role will be much more important than "what you know" about assigning, writing business plans, or holding your team accountable. Success is a choice, so read on and start enjoying the benefits of maintaining a **Mindset of Success**.

Call Me KOWISO, Because I Know One When I See One!

Situation:

Bill's track record as a producer was second to none, clearly showing he had what it took to rack up sales numbers. After five successive years of being the company's top producer, Bill made The Leap, went out on his own and opened his own sales agency. For three years he operated on a shoestring to keep expenses low and to build a cash reserve for future growth. As his business grew, so did the need for a skilled salesperson that could deliver the combination of great numbers and the right touch of personal service for his customers.

"How hard can it be, finding a suitable performer?" Bill thought to himself, recalling that he had little training and experience when he first started in sales. There must be a ton of qualified people with enough product knowledge to keep the customers happy and keep sales numbers climbing at the same time. Bill was certain of this and said to himself, "I Know One When I See One," but after four tries and four failures, Bill didn't know what to do or where to start looking next.

Diagnosis:

In every profession, resumes can often create as many problems as they solve. No one ever writes that they aren't competent, won't tolerate long hours, hate traveling, never actually finished that course, or have a hard time getting along with customers and co-workers. No, every resume declares that the candidate is a brilliant or, at bare minimum, a highly competent, trained professional that can deliver the goods for your organization.

Like many entrepreneurs, Bill thought he knew exactly what kind of person he needed to add to the sales team. Using his experience as a top producer, Bill figured he could pick a winner with ease and avoid the problem of not having enough manpower to cover the growing territory. But Bill did what many entrepreneurs and sales managers do every day when hiring: They look at the resume as gospel and then don't do the real work needed to successfully hire a new team member.

Prescription:

Keeping any organization adequately staffed requires more than running ads, reading resumes, and conducting interviews. Bill, a highly successful sales professional, allowed his lack of hiring experience to override the real need to investigate references, conduct sufficient background checks, and validate a candidate's real will to be successful in sales.

There are hiring processes that work and hiring processes that essentially create bigger problems than they fix. By using outsourced services, or at least using instruments that uncover what resumes and interviews won't reveal about a candidate, Bill may have avoided the frustration of repeatedly hiring people that didn't work out. In short, it is essential to have a process that is more powerful than the person charged with getting the hiring right.

I Love That Guy's Work, But I Just Don't Like Him

Situation:

Jamal felt stuck and didn't like his options. One of the top performers on his sales team left him confused every time they traveled together. At the end of trip, there was always a long list of PO's to turn in to the shipping department, but Jamal just didn't like spending time with this top performer. He was certain that one of his gifts as a manager was his intuition about people, but he couldn't figure this guy out. How could he feel so disconnected from someone that showed true skill at getting the job done?

Diagnosis:

Like many managers or team leaders, Jamal had a blind spot in his managerial talent for truly understanding behavioral gifts. If he had taken the time to review history, Jamal probably would have discovered the pattern of people, like this current employee, that found convenient reasons to leave the team despite consistent performance.

Jamal tended to surround himself with players that fit his style, even if they weren't the best of the bunch as far as getting things done. These were people Jamal got along with easily, so he tended to believe they were doing what he would do out in the field.

Besides, Jamal was good enough to get promoted to the top position, so how wrong could that practice be anyway?

Prescription:

In many cases, the people Jamal felt comfortable managing were people that helped him feel good about himself. This group wanted his attention, wanted his help on sales calls, tended to push decisions back to Jamal, and only moved as far as he allowed them to. Jamal needs to remember what it means to be a manager: Get top performance out of your team.

Jamal first needs to understand Behavioral Styles to better communicate and understand his employees' performances. Second, letting go of his urge to be the Promoter for everyone would allow Jamal to turn this high performer loose to pursue his own goals. Instead of worrying about why he could not get comfortable with his team member, Jamal needs to go back to school and become better at providing the support that all of his people need. Different is not wrong, it is just different. Jamal has been confusing style differences with performance capability.

My People Love Me, So Why Won't They Sell For Me?

Situation:

Ronald and his team seemed to be in an eternal love fest. They celebrated everyone's birthday or other significant life event, and the harmony on the team could not have been smoother. Unlike some of the other managers at his level, Ron's relationships with his team were more like friendships than boss/employer. After having worked for a manager that treated everyone like a cog in the machine rather than a person, Ron vowed never to behave in that fashion with his subordinates. You could often hear people saying they'd die if Ron ever left the company or was replaced for any reason. It was all good, except the numbers never hit the targets despite how much everyone was happy to be working for a boss like Ron.

Diagnosis:

The balancing act many managers never seem to master is the one that keeps business and friendships in line. Ron worked so hard to be the good guy everyone wanted as a boss that he had blurred the lines between boss and pal. When the results didn't show up, Ron had become so invested in the sales team as people that he couldn't bring himself to hold anyone accountable or not get caught up in his belief they were all working hard enough to succeed. Ron wanted to be liked more than he wanted to be a real boss.

Prescription:

Certainly there are many tales of bosses that go too far on the other side of this story. Dictatorial leaders often become victims of friendly fire, or sales teams that figure out how to get the boss fired for their poor performance. All managers must remember that their number one responsibility is producing results, and establishing the authority to make those results happen is essential. First, be clear about expectations regarding performance. Second, always have consequences when people fall below the baseline of acceptable performance. Third, be consistent and self-sustaining, and that typically means not getting your emotional needs met from your subordinates. Nurturing the person will generally produce a higher-performing employee, but expecting them to produce because they like you will generally not support long-term managerial success.

Is Honesty Always The Best Policy?

Situation:

Geoff hated reading poor performance reports. As the manager of a large, inside sales/customer service team, Geoff found himself facing data that didn't lie: One third of his team was consistently below the baseline expectation for call volume handled and add-on sales generated. What made the situation worse was that upper management was now paying particular attention to Geoff's department's metrics and looking for his plan for getting the numbers trending upward again. If things didn't improve over the next quarter, Geoff was certain cuts would be necessary. Rather than tell his people the real story, he continually soft-peddled the message, believing that his team could read between the lines and pick up the pace. The quarter came and went, no significant changes were apparent, and not only did 20% of his people get pink slipped, Geoff found himself out on the street as well.

Diagnosis:

Geoff is guilty of letting his behavioral style get in the way of his and his team's success. By hoping his people would get the message, Geoff actually created an environment that allowed them to deny any individual responsibility for their performances. Geoff liked his people and didn't want to scare any of them with the message from upper management, so he avoided having the appropriate conversations with all of them until the message was the last one he wanted to deliver: You no longer work here.

Prescription:

Managing requires Adult/Adult conversations take place regularly and effectively. Yes, these can be uncomfortable when people aren't performing as expected, but not telling people the truth about where they stand is irresponsible. Developing the skills and implementing processes that create honest appraisal and course correction are essential for anyone leading teams. Believing your team members all want to do the right things is acceptable, but believing that everyone knows exactly what the right actions are is not acceptable. Never allow your people to operate without clearly defined expectations, and just as Hope is not a sales strategy and Hope is not a management tool.

Should You Really Have An Open Door Policy? Being Available Isn't Always Good.

Situation:

When Mike was introduced as the new regional manager at the company's quarterly meeting, he proudly declared, "I have an open door policy with all of my people." Mike made sure that everyone knew he would be around whenever needed, and the only thing necessary to reach him was to knock on the door and walk into his office. What could be a better way to open a good line of communication and show how committed his was to working with this new team? However, when Mike got his evaluation at the end of his first 90 days, the boss's comments about not seeing the progress he had expected shook Mike up. His team was happy, but things weren't going well.

Diagnosis:

Like many managers who want to be there for the team, Mike's situation is happening in companies all over the map. Mike is so busy "being available" that he isn't capable of getting his own work accomplished. Mike fell into the trap of becoming a bottleneck rather than a driver for his region since no one felt compelled to make decisions on their own anymore. The team started taking everything through Mike's open door and let him make the final call about even the most trivial of issues. Mike's team loved him because he paid attention to them but also because he was doing all their work as well.

Prescription:

Many managers pride themselves on offering an open door to their teams. In theory, this strategy seems like a positive way to stay connected to your people, let them know you care, and catch problems before they spin out of control. On the other hand, that open door policy can become an open invitation for people to dump their unwanted work or responsibilities on the boss's desk. Very little good can come from a situation where the manager's duties are always taking a back seat to those of the people he or she is leading. The boss is going to end up doing more work than he or she is able to and consequently taking the blame when goals aren't met or assignments aren't completed.

Use a calendar to manage your work and to manage the access that your people have to you. This way, you can set the priorities for leading instead of being pulled down into the lower level work that your people are responsible for accomplishing. Don't let the fear of being unavailable overpower the need to get things done. Once your team learns how you operate, the system will work for everyone.

Have You Made Enough Deposits To Cover That Withdrawal?

Situation:

Known as a taskmaster, Gerald surveyed the numbers in the mid-year sales reports and decided it was time to light a fire under his troops. Despite his constant drilling them for call reports and his black and white assessment of what he heard and read, Gerald was not able to understand why the numbers were less than ideal. There was no way he could let the team slip further behind the goals set at the beginning of the year.

So at the next sales meeting, no one escaped Gerald's wrath. He blasted each of them for being lazy, uncommitted, stupid, or taking up valuable space that someone else would like to have on his team. To say it was ugly was an understatement, and his sales team couldn't wait to get out of that room as quickly as possible.

But what happened next really caught Gerald off guard, for three letters of resignation had been slipped under his door by 8:00 the next morning. Gerald did want to get a reaction, but this wasn't what he anticipated when he "challenged" his team to step up and perform.

Diagnosis:

Any way you look at it, Gerald's performance was less than appropriate when dealing with a team of adults. Some managers think that instilling fear or calling people names sends the message that improvement must be made. Some feel that "heads will roll" is a great motivator, and apparently, Gerald is one of these people. What happened had really started months before, and the three team members that left were already thinking about looking for work elsewhere. Gerald didn't believe that positive strokes were effective in long-term management success. On the contrary, he felt that belittling people or questioning their professionalism or commitment would keep people producing. He did pay attention to his sales force, but it was always negative, and he had finally pushed too far with his last tirade.

Prescription:

The most effective managers learn that keeping their people connected and productive requires making deposits in everyone's emotional bank account. By handing out genuine strokes for performance and for effort, Gerald might have accumulated enough credit to make a big withdrawal when he asked for it. Unfortunately for him, Gerald's balance with his people was so low that when he blew up, he overdrew his account with at least three team members. They no longer had any faith that he saw them as people, and they thought that he only cared about whether or not he'd look good as a sales manager when the numbers came out. Managers must always be concerned about making the necessary deposits in their team's accounts, for if not, there may be nothing left to draw upon when they need it most.

Don't Let Climbing The Ladder Make You Less Aware

Situation:

Everyone in the company was happy to see Michael get the promotion to Senior VP of Sales. For years, Michael had been a loyal employee and had always taken time to help others whenever he could. He seemed to have a great feel for when others needed a pat on the back or someone to listen to them. Michael's career started as a college intern, and then moved on to inside sales. His long and very successful stint as a top producer on the outside sales team appeared to be the reason he was rewarded with the new title.

But what happened over the next few months took everyone by surprise. The caring, compassionate Michael morphed into a number crunching, spec-sheet quoting machine that had little time for any of the people that cheered so loudly when he got the promotion. In short, Michael had become robotic in his day-to-day dealings with everyone around him. No one liked it, including some of the old customers he had stayed in touch with. And these people were now complaining about his new, business-only demeanor.

Diagnosis:

Michael forgot how much of his success was linked to the relationships he had formed with everyone throughout his career. When he ascended to the new Senior VP role, there seemed to be a subconscious message that told Michael to prove how smart he was and to not rely on his people skills to succeed at this new level of responsibility and authority. If he could impress with numbers and product knowledge, he would most assuredly be seen as a great leader and resource. Michael now believed that his IQ was more important than his EQ.

Prescription:

Understanding yourself at any point in time is valuable, and there are a myriad of tools and assessments to help anyone become more conscious of how they are interacting with others. In the medical field, this sense of self is often called "bedside manner," and doctors that have both tremendous skills as a physician and good bedside manners are what we all desire. Michael needs to spend some time developing his personal awareness by having his Emotional Intelligence tested, reviewing the results, and committing to plan of action to stay connected to the people that he used to have cheering for him. Along with his EQ, understanding his Behavioral Style and Personal Motivators might help Michael become an even more dynamic leader and help him win back all of those once raving fans that now believe he had gotten too big for his britches.

The Power of Punctuation

Situation:

Having just arrived from his job at a competitor, Stew was settling in as the new Regional Sales Manager at Plumbing Parts and Pieces, Inc. For the first week or so, he was content to observe the culture and get familiar with his new surroundings, and he had started to meet and interact with his new sales team. Nothing was more important than establishing his credibility and authority with these guys that he had worked so hard to outsell for the last 15 years. Telling them how he used to do things and how his ideas were better than what he saw his new team practicing, Stew was sure they would see the benefit of having him as an asset at PPP, Inc. instead of an adversary at his old firm. Sadly, after the first few weeks of cordiality, the new team seemed to disconnect from Stew, leaving him wondering if he had made a bad choice to accept the new position. Over the next couple of months, the situation got worse and the relationships remained icy at best.

Diagnosis:

Stew got caught in a common mistake that many new managers make when they join a new company or take over a new team. Stew felt he had to TELL everyone how good he was instead of letting them figure it out, and in doing so, the exact opposite of what he hoped to accomplish happened. In his efforts to show off his smarts and authority, Stew lost track of how powerful and nurturing asking questions can be for a manager. Stew opted to make declarations about his selling and managerial prowess, fearful that if he did ask questions, he might be perceived as timid or unqualified. "Questions are for the weak, and no one wants to work for a weak manager," was Stew's mindset as he approached this new position at his former competitor.

Prescription:

There is a lot of pressure to establish credibility when a manager takes over a new team, and the instinct to declare that credibility is natural. However, the existing team may have been very successful before a new manager arrived, and by trying to demand respect, Stew actually pushed his people away. Asking to get rescued with questions that start with phrases like "can you help me with how you guys typically handle this?" or "I see that your processes are different, so what is the most important part of this that I should focus on first?" will allow the team members to feel appreciated and unthreatened by the new comer. Question marks are powerful punctuation and sprinkling them throughout your normal conversation can be very nurturing and often opens up an opportunity for both parties to learn about one another. Telling is often the last thing a new team wants from a new leader. By being strategically deaf, dumb, and confused, anyone can appear less demanding and more approachable.

SECTION 2
Activity

SECTION 2
Activity

Just as any successful manager must hold the team accountable for doing the basic activities that generate the company's desired results, a manager must be held accountable for performing fundamental activities of team and personnel supervision. Evaluating team members, providing support and coaching, defining goals, reviewing performance, and effective hiring are all components of a manager's performance requirements. No matter what size of the organization you are operating in, there is no excuse for letting any of these elements of success to be ignored. Successful leadership is a matter of eliminating as many surprises as possible. When you commit to performing these activities on a regular basis, the job can be much less stressful and much more predictable.

At its core, successful management of people is the art of knowing why things are going well, why things might not be going well, and how to get people back on track when course corrections are required. No remote control management practice works well for very long, so committing to a consistent set of activities that keeps you tuned in to your team is essential. "No news is good news" isn't necessarily true when we are talking about managing a team. No news might mean everyone's left the team, if you aren't careful.

Managers must be accountable for these activities. Admittedly, people can be messy whether they try to be or not. Therefore, some of these activities are not always pleasant, and procrastinating about them is always a temptation when the "kids" are acting up. High level team performance is not accidental, so every manager that wants to maximize the team's potential must make sure these activities are regularly scheduled components of their work.

This chapter helps you avoid the behavior of a college student who cuts class all semester and then crams the night before the final exam to try to get a passing grade. When the latest sales reports come out and the numbers are lagging, many managers attempt to manage when it is too late. Make these activities the cornerstone of your success no matter what the sales numbers indicate.

If You Don't Inspect It, You Can't Expect It

Situation:

Ellen was feeling stuck, frustrated, and totally helpless. Once again, despite telling her team how important it was to communicate the new shipping terms and fees to her sales force, the complaints from her customers about not getting any warning would not cease. Ellen knew that push back was inevitable when headquarters decide to tighten up on the freight allowances, and the evidence now made it clear that none of her team had delivered the message. How could she enforce the new policies without risking a mass exodus of customers? How did she get caught in this trap after all of her people said they would take care of this critical issue?

Diagnosis:

Like so many other managers, Ellen wants to believe her people understand the gravity and importance of situations like these. So when she called a staff meeting to inform everyone from the new directive from the home office, Ellen thought the matter had been handled. Since there was no pushback from her people, why should she have felt the need to monitor the commitment? Ellen made the serious mistake of not establishing a way to report back. Receiving feedback on how the word was being passed on the new shipping policy would have allowed her to verify the message had been delivered as well as measure the customers' reaction to the hike in fees. Ellen didn't do the tough part of the assignment, and neither did her people.

Prescription:

Because many people would rather avoid confrontation or delivering bad news like an adult, all managers must insist on a report back step. Getting surprised when there is no time to course correct creates another problem that typically dwarfs the original challenge. Never believe that your people have what it takes to deal with tough circumstances. Take full responsibility for the work getting done by requiring that everyone be accountable for proving the mission was accomplished.

The Pipeline Is Full, But The Results Are Lacking

Situation:

Rachel's sense of dread began to build when she looked at her planner and noticed it was almost the end of the month. Every thirty days she was required to have a "pipeline review meeting," a get-together that was certainly not the highlight on anyone's calendar. Rachel had even heard this confab referred to as "Black Friday," and not because people was getting good news about the sales results from the previous month. At every one of the monthly meetings, upper management required sales team members to present their current pipeline and project the sales for the next 90 days. And each month, management would ask why these glowing reports didn't ever match up with the sales that were actually being won.

Diagnosis:

This situation happens in sales departments all across the landscape. Salespeople want to look busy and sound optimistic, so they load up the pipeline with anyone who has expressed the least bit of interest in buying anything, no matter how small or when the sale might happen. In an effort to avoid being exposed as active but not productive, salespeople actually create a much bigger problem by telling a tale that will never come true. Sales managers must stop this practice and insist on accurate projections of business.

Prescription:

To facilitate a pipeline review that's remotely accurate, Rachel and other sales managers like her must count the things that matter most as far as sales process activities, and then they must learn how to read between the lines to see what those numbers are actually telling them. In order to make this work, managers must teach this type of disciplined analysis to their sales team so they can become more aware of their actual production and how this information can then be used to forecast future success.

Many sales people don't disqualify enough opportunities, many times believing that breathing is all a prospect needs to do to be a real opportunity. High-performing sales management insists that producers can justify the value of the work and provide reliable data to their supervisors.

Delegation: Problem Solver or Nightmare Creator?

Situation:

The workload had been backing up on Dottie's desk for the last month, and now she could barely see over the stacks of folders that were not getting the attention they required. Despite having a staff that was more than willing, Dottie kept thinking that no one could do the work as well as she could. Even worse, she feared that if she did choose to delegate some of it, no one would finish and return the assignments by the deadlines she was facing. So once again, the midnight oil would be burning, and Dottie would feel overworked, frustrated, and under-appreciated for the effort she put forth. She could feel the stress building, but anxiety over problems that delegating might create left her paralyzed, a victim of her own processes.

Diagnosis:

Dottie was correct. She did do the work better than anyone on her staff, but that didn't mean she should do everything that comes her way. With a serious case of Self-Limiting Beliefs defining how valuable or effective delegating could be in times like this, Dottie continued to bury herself with deadlines and long hours. Dottie probably learned about delegating early in her career when a boss behaved the same way, so she came to believe that spreading the work around was more trouble than it was worth. Why risk getting caught by that mistake if she could avoid it, even if it meant a being a boss that never went home?

Prescription:

Delegation is an essential tool for any successful leader or team manager. The problem is most managers never learn how to delegate effectively. There are some critical components that Dottie needed to learn if she were ever to escape her self-inflicted pain. First, change the belief that her time is worth more than the workers down line. Second, learn that effective delegation requires giving the right directions, expectations, follow-up instructions, and deadlines to the right person. Third, Dottie has to change her view on how valuable delegating can be for long-term development of her team and her employees. Showing you trust someone with a critical task can accelerate that worker's growth and perception of how good he or she are at the job. Finally, Dottie must accept that in the beginning, delegating will take a little longer for each task to be completed, but in the long run and in the big picture, her life as a manager will be much more satisfying and much less stressful.

How Long Does It Take To Change The Numbers?

Situation:

Really Big Equipment Company hired Bob to turn the sales team around. Bob was an experienced sales manager with many years of industry experience and a reputation as a "get it done" type of guy. The CEO of RBEC called Bob into his office on his first day and told him that there was no time to get comfortable. Investors were starting to get concerned about the company's performance, so Bob needed to show some big results immediately. Bob heard the message and was about to ask the CEO some critical questions, but before that could happen, the CEO shook his hand and headed to his golf outing. Bob headed back to his office and called his wife, explaining that for the first time in his career, he might be facing failure.

Diagnosis:

The CEO displayed how little he knew about the day-to-day operations or sales processes at Really Big Equipment Company. By telling Bob that results had to appear immediately, if not sooner, the CEO showed that he never dared to think about what it really took to generate one sale, let alone construct a consistent run of growing revenue. Bob may have stepped into a job that was set up for failure. His reputation as a high-performing sales manager had been forged at organizations that understood sales cycles and closing percentages. This new position had no margin for error or time to ramp up to success.

Prescription:

Every organization must understand the realities of its market and the truth about the sales cycles that are in play. Sales success in most business-to-business situations requires managing a sales process that takes time, rather than one that closes the deal on one call. Really Big Equipment's typical sale took three to four months and required a salesperson to meet with several people on the prospect side of the opportunity. Bob and the CEO need to get on the same page about what are reasonable expectations regarding producing immediate results. They have to evaluate the sales pipeline realistically, analyze any current open opportunities, assess the length of their sales cycle, and then come to an agreement regarding how soon revenues can improve. Just demanding results *now* is rarely the right formula for turning any numbers around.

Are All These Meetings Really Necessary?

Situation:

John looked at his Outlook calendar and saw another of those meetings coming up that just made him ask, "Are all these meetings necessary?" It seemed his manager would call the team together for any reason that came to mind, like a customer called to say his shipment was late, the home office was thinking about a new logo, the vacation calendar had just been posted or a search was beginning for a new accounting clerk.

All John wanted was to do his job, creating great relationships with good clients that ordered lots of product. All these meetings seemed to get in the way of John doing what he thought the company was paying him to do, and his attitude was beginning to show some strain. The number of meetings scheduled at the last minute was creating another challenge, for his clients were getting tired of John having to cancel the meetings he had set with them, and those valuable relationships were beginning to fray a bit.

Diagnosis:

Many managers have the best intentions when scheduling meetings to keep the team informed of what is going on with the business or in the office. The struggle arises when the team starts to see no value in convening other than having a manager wishing to be seen as a manager. Or, even worse, all the extra meetings become time bandits that get in the way of actually producing results.

By opting to let everyone know as much about everything through the use of meetings, good managers actually devalue the time they expect the team to protect and use wisely. Improper use of meetings can be as dangerous as not having any meetings at all.

Prescription:

Meetings are for decisions, not discussions. Use appropriate tools to send out appropriate information. Save those scheduled meetings for essential actions and decisions that require all invitees to be engaged. Spending your time assets to build morale or send out updates rarely qualify for a scheduled meeting with your entire team. Email and voice mail rule those situations, particularly if the targeted audience is one or two people rather than the whole staff. Follow these rules and gain effectiveness in your meetings and save time for everyone:

1. Have an agenda with decisions to be made and not just talked about.

2. Set time limits and stick to them. Start and stop on the appointed times.

3. Review, recap, and remind with everyone in attendance to make sure the meeting accomplished your goals.

4. Assign pre-meeting work to those that are best suited to deliver when the time comes. Eliminate an all-votes-matter attitude. Someone will always be unhappy.

5. Use the beginning and end of the day if at all possible.

6. Use the event to acknowledge successes, but save discipline for private conversations.

The Worst Time To Dig A Well Is When You Are Thirsty

Situation:

Abby dreaded hiring new sales people. The process of sourcing qualified candidates, scheduling interviews, having candidates cancel or not even show up for those interviews, and making job offers that were not accepted was enough to send Abby out for a bottle of Tums. There was only one thing that could be worse though, and that was having to fill a critical position NOW, which was exactly the position she found herself in. Abby was forced to let a territory rep go just as the company was about to launch a hot new product, and she knew that upper management would not be happy at all if every territory was not fully covered with proven performers. One bottle of Tums might not be enough as she had to prepare sales presentations, approve all the collateral materials, design a sales plan and work up six-month projections, all the while trying to beat the bushes in search of a top-level sales person.

Diagnosis:

Old habits die hard, and Abby's process of seeking new talent has her in a real pickle. Like many sales managers, Abby believes that recruiting personnel only takes place when you have an opening to fill on the sales team. There are so many other important tasks and job requirements to take care of, so Abby never thought about what would happen if the perfect storm appeared. Why go through all that unnecessary aggravation if there isn't a job to offer? Well, the clouds were starting to gather and Abby felt like failure was inevitable.

Prescription:

You can never have too many resumes to read, and when all she needed was just one, Abby had nothing. What Abby failed to consider is that hiring takes time, and by not having an active and on-going recruiting process, there was no one "on the bench" to help her when this crisis hit. The best managers realize that you can't always predict when a job opening will appear on the team. In order to not get caught shorthanded, they are always looking for more and better talent to add to their sales forces. Even if you can't make someone an offer, the discipline of regularly interviewing and staying in touch with candidates can provide you with a steady source of potential employees. Hiring a winner is hard enough without the added pressure of having a short time line to get it done right. The worst time to be looking for water is when you're too thirsty to dig the well.

The Right Language Helps Hit Goals

Situation:

After reviewing the last quarter's sales figures, Alex knew his team was on track to hit the annual sales quota that the VP of Sales had mandated. Three of his people were killing it, five were steady if not spectacular, and the final two needed just a little attention to get back on track. All in all, the team was performing well, and Alex felt good about how his management style was working with everyone.

The next team meeting was just around the corner, and Alex planned on being totally honest with the group. He would go over their individual and collective performances, but he also wanted to see if he could get even more out of them. So, in an even tone that was neither critical nor demanding, Alex told them that the numbers could be better, that he'd like to see better results and that some of them needed to work harder. When he was finished, every one nodded that they understood the message and headed back to work.

Certain that he had given them all the push they needed, Alex was surprised that the next quarter's number showed no bump or movement towards more sales revenue. "What happened?" was all Alex could think as he looked at the disappointing numbers.

Diagnosis:

Alex had the right intention when he spoke to his team at that meeting. He wanted to push a little but not sound like he was criticizing the good performances that were there. In his effort to be nurturing while at the same time sharing his desire to see even stronger results, Alex believed that the words he chose were enough to convey his message. But his language wasn't clear, and his vagueness left no one exactly sure what Alex wanted them to do after the meeting. What precisely did he mean by wanting to see "better numbers" or for them to all "work harder"? As simple as it might sound, fuzzy wording is often just enough to inspire people to not screw up instead of striving for more.

Prescription:

When you give people clear and specific goals, their decision making and commitment can be tied to a defined outcome, not a vague and often misunderstood definition of "more" or "better." Was "better" one more closed deal? Was "working harder" spending more hours driving around the territory? Provide your people with clear outcomes to work towards so there is no question as to what you expect. Ask for 10% more revenue instead of better numbers. Tell people you want prospecting numbers to go up five more calls per week instead of working harder. When it can be measured and quantified, the results will follow. Use the right, specific language to clarify your expectations.

Who's Problem Is It Anyway?

Situation:

Mark and Tony were at it again, and Phyllis, their sales manager, was about to get caught in the middle one more time. Phyllis had fallen victim to this scenario before, where two employees had developed a problem and had refused to work it out for themselves. For some reason, her best efforts to help these two "children" learn to share always ended up with Phyllis taking the blame for disappointing one of them. This time, Mark and Tony had both helped advance a sales process all the way to completion, but now they were arguing over how to split the commission. Neither wanted to figure out a compromise, and all Phyllis could do was sigh as she heard the two of them coming down the hall calling to her, "You have to do something, Phyllis…"

Diagnosis:

Many managers take the job believing that they must be judge and jury in situations like the one Phyllis is facing. In reality, these two "children," are not being adult enough to just make a decision they both can live with and settle the issue. By dragging Phyllis into their sandbox, Mark and Tony are taking her time away from any real issues that may need her attention. Instead,

Phyllis has been snared by not requiring her team members do their work and making them take ownership of their problem. She can't win with one of them for sure and will most likely disappoint both parties one way or another.

Prescription:

Phyllis needed to set the rules for this circumstance as soon as she hired any new team members. There could be no uncertainty about what would happen if two adults refused to take ownership of a situation and solve a problem like this for themselves. Here is a story of how one successful CEO established his rules for just this scenario: Roger Staubach, former NFL great and now a highly successful business owner, brought two squabbling salespeople into his office to listen to each plead his case for the lion's share of a sales commission. After hearing both sides, Staubach asked what the total amount was that the sale netted both the salespeople and the company. Once he verified the information, Staubach made an unusual decision, one that unambiguously stated things like this should never reach his desk again. He took the entire commission—including the company's share—and donated it to charity and in doing so let no one "win" the argument. From that moment forward, no one has ever let a disagreement get to the point where a resolution could not be reached.

Phyllis must take a similar course of action and make a similar statement to be sure everyone knows how she will resolve these problems before it happens again.

SECTION 3
Process

SECTION 3
Process

How often have we heard a battle-hardened leader explain his success by saying, "I don't know how I do it, but whatever I do seems to work?" That lack of understanding creates a number of problems for both the manager and his team.

For this type of manager, the lack of awareness of his tactical maneuvers will leave him floundering and frustrated when that behavior doesn't work consistently. How can he fix something when he cannot honestly identify what might be broken in the first place? The team suffers when eager young people have to be mentored or trained by the more senior team member that cannot identify what really works or what really doesn't.

Leadership should never be a game played on automatic pilot. True professionals develop skills and processes that allow them to operate effectively when communicating with the team, evaluating performance, disciplining people, and hiring new team members. Using a consistent process and knowing where you are in that process will allow you to manage yourself to success, and truly get out of the habit of "flying by the seat of your pants" leadership.

This chapter includes tactics and process management tools that you may be familiar with. However, what we have found over the years is that far too many managers don't know how, when, or why they should utilize these tools. Our goal is for you to develop the awareness, as well as the tactical proficiency, that a strong management process can provide.

Moving Your Team Up The Level Of Effort Ladder

Situation:

Tara was at her wit's end as she did the end of year assessments of her team. The profit goals were hit, the sales trends were positive, and all of her people made more this year than last, but something was bothering her. What could be causing the angst and frustration to build in this manager's mind? Tara's self-review opened her eyes to the realization that most of what her team had accomplished had come at the expense of her time and energy. The longer Tara looked at her notes on the entire team's performance, she found herself asking the same question: "If I am the manager, why am I always doing everyone else's work on top of all of mine?"

Diagnosis:

Like many managers, Tara has trouble keeping her team's world out of her world. Tara is certainly committed to success, even if it means she would do all the things her downline people could not or would not take responsibility for. Tara developed the mind set that just jumping in and saving the day was easier than forcing her team members to learn to perform better or going out and finding new members. Tara's situation was no one's fault but her own, and it was a dilemma that many managers find themselves in before they realize just how much it costs.

Prescription:

When the situation above occurs, it is often created by no one other than the manager herself. Tara needs to go back and re-establish the Levels of Effort with her team members again:

1. **That's not my job:** A position incorporating the least amount of expectation and engagement.

2. **What should I do?:** Requires constant direction and course correction by the manager.

3. **Here is what I think I should do:** An engaged and proactive level of performance that contributes to the thought process of success.

4. **Here is what I just did:** Ownership of their work and thoughts, and now taking personal initiative. This still engages manager, but after the fact.

5. **Oh, by the way:** Total accountability and personal responsibility. This person has a track record of good decision making and can work autonomously.

Some salespeople find taking the path of least resistance safer than moving up to a position of self-responsibility and accountability. Tara would like to believe she has elevated her team to the 4th Level, where they make decisions and report the outcomes.

The team, however, feels Tara wants them to operate at the 2nd Level which still requires a manager to be highly involved. With regular Personal Evaluation Interviews, Tara can get her team members back on track so she can return to leading the team instead of doing the lion's share of their work.

Evaluations: Why Isn't Once A Year Enough?

Situation:

The now ex-employee had "that look" which Sarah had seen too often before. Sarah had just done one of the hardest things a manager or business owner has to do when she let Mike go last Thursday. What Sarah hated about the look was that it told her the Mike was totally surprised he had gotten the axe. As far as Mike knew, his performance was on par with what was expected by his employer. And besides, his evaluation just ten months ago had but two comments about his occasionally arriving late at his desk.

Diagnosis:

Sarah's situation is common in the workplace. Employees are typically evaluated annually, if at all, and are given little information on how they are really performing. Management hands out a report card once a year that is often little more than a polite exercise which either leaves the employee wondering why they didn't get a raise or, worse, delivers nothing more than the message there is little management wants to talk with them about. How was Mike to know he was being measured on a performance that might lead to his dismissal if he didn't make the grade? How was he to know what that grade was? When employees with good attitudes turn sour, it is typically the manager's fault for not conveying the proper message in the proper time frame. People generally want to be positive performers, so management must implement tools to accommodate that wish.

Prescription:

Regular and consistent Personal Evaluation Interviews are necessary to stop the surprises. When an employee gets a regular paycheck, it leads them to believe they're doing what management wants. By implementing an objective and collaborative process which requires managers to hold employees accountable for improvement and to support that improvement, the Sarahs and Mikes of the world can avoid those surprising outcomes everyone dreads. It's necessary for employees to understand the level of performance they are delivering in the work place, and it's necessary for management to keep them informed on how they're doing. Trusting employees to remember everything they were told in the annual review cheats them of the opportunity to take ownership of the condition and often allows the manager to relinquish the responsibility of improving the individual's and the team's performance.

Why Do I Have To Tell Everyone Three Times What I Want Done?

Situation:

The big presentation was due on Monday morning, and Martin had given everyone their assignments two weeks in advance. Now, as he sat in his office pulling his hair out wondering why all the data and analysis was not turned in yet, all Martin could imagine was getting thrown out of the senior managers' conference. Surely his team was not trying to set him up for failure, but why didn't they understand how important the schedule was to Martin? Everyone knows this is the make-or-break meeting of the year, and the team should have had everything ready long before now. That goes without saying, doesn't it?

Diagnosis:

Leaving a conversation unfinished is a cardinal sin when managing a group. Sure, Martin's team knew how important that meeting was for him, but everything this company asked of its workforce seemed to have "urgent" written all over it. Martin believed that his priorities did not require a special comment or note of expectation. Now that the deadline was looming and Martin felt impending doom, he couldn't imagine that he had any reason to question his management process. Martin kept wanting to believe that his team was the problem, not his management skill or tactics.

Prescription:

All managers can probably recall a situation like Martin's. Understanding Levels of Trust is the key ingredient in eliminating the recurring nightmare of not getting projects done on time. Martin told people what he wanted but failed to tell them how or when he wanted them to be involved. By learning the 5 Levels of Trust and Accountability, mentioned earlier in "Moving Your Team Up the Level of Effort Ladder," Martin could make sure his team met his expectations before any problems came up. Expecting Level 3 performance from Level 1 employees is a recipe for disaster. Martin needs to stop expecting people to change their performance when he has not trained them how to meet his expectations.

Motivation: Isn't That Part Of My Job?

Situation:

August had arrived, and all of the sales team looked like they'd much rather be sipping umbrella drinks on the beach instead of grinding through the phone blitz promoting the new product offering. As Regional Sales Manager, Charlie heard how de-energized everyone sounded and decided to jump right into action by delivering a fire and brimstone speech about the great opportunity the company was providing everyone and what a great place to work XYZ, Inc. had become over the last few years. Certainly the passion and subliminal message about "do it or else" would turn the tide and get everyone back on track. Charlie possessed the gift to inspire, but as he left the room, the grumbling had already started and the mood remained sour.

Diagnosis:

Although every manager needs to be able to help people when times are tough or they just need a boost, Charlie had become too caught up in believing he knew how to reach anyone with his emotional pleas and his "little engine that could" analogies. So whenever the sales force appeared disinterested, you could always count on Charlie to put on a show. He believed that the fear of losing a job could always be tapped to restart the troops. In his mind, Charlie was a world-class motivator, but his people had another opinion.

Prescription:

Too many managers think employees come to work for the same reasons they do, and therefore default to delivering a message that resonates with their own values and motivators. Understanding that people act for their own reasons and no one else's is a fundamental managerial requirement. Whether it is to make money to buy a new home, feel the magic of helping others, growing intellectually, or becoming a team leader, a manager must know how to connect to the motivations that people bring to the workplace. Creating a nurturing environment that allows workers to connect their efforts to these personal values is more effective than learning how to crack the whip, threaten termination, or dangle a few bonus dollars for chasing a goal.

Everyone Loves A Year-End Bonus, Don't They?

Situation:

Raj inspected the year-end numbers and couldn't believe what the data was telling him. Not one of his producers qualified for the year-end bonus that he asked the CFO to include in the compensation plan he designed. He was stunned at how the opportunity to make an extra 5-7% of their annual earnings could not inspire the sales team to do a little more. Having an extra check could possibly pay for a nice weekend away somewhere or maybe even ease some college tuition stresses he knew were burdening some members of his team.

Diagnosis:

Performance-based pay plans often motivate employees, but plans that only reward once a year typically don't have much impact. Humans like to see results in much shorter time spans, and Raj's plan created too long a wait between action and reward. By the end of the third quarter, most people had figured out whether they would qualify for the bonus or not, and if not, there was no use in going after the prize. Instead, they hit cruise control and did just enough to not get any negative recognition.

Prescription:

Designing performance-based compensation plans is one of the biggest challenges in the business world today. What level of production is expected for the base pay can be a difficult calculation, and trying to figure out what is actually attainable beyond that can be even more perplexing. This is all further complicated because employees tend to find a way to "game" every comp plan.

So what really works? There are a couple of rules that should be applied to any base comp plan and any bonus plan. First and foremost, all compensation plans should be created to reward the behavior and results that accomplish the company's goals. Comp plans must be clear from the very beginning, with relatively few moving parts or ambiguous standards. All bonus structures or "above and beyond" components should align with the first two points mentioned here. They should be offered quarterly so there is enough short-term impact to change behavior or actively engage an employee to attain the reward. Other than that, your compensation plans might just be telling people to find a comfortable level of production and don't risk shooting for the stars and then failing.

Leading, Managing, Or Administrating, Pick One

Situation:

Ernest, VP of Sales, was preparing for his company's annual sales meeting. In reviewing the results of the six territories that reported to him, Ernest was struggling to find consistency in how he was going to approach the performance reviews of the six different Sales Directors. Some of them had hit their sales goals perfectly. Some of the Sales Directors just missed their numbers but had all the call reports anyone could ask for, all neatly filed throughout the year. And some of these Sales Directors had a long way to go to meet their goals, but their paperwork was amazing, with projections and progress reports and market analyses so rich you'd think they couldn't have missed the mark. What was going on that six people could do the same job in so many different ways?

Diagnosis:

Like many high-level executives, Ernest wasn't aware of how well job expectations, roles, and responsibilities were explained to the people below him in the corporate hierarchy. Didn't everyone with the title of "Sales Director" know how to do that position well and up to the company's expectations? Ernest just assumed the job meant the same thing to each of the six people that reported to him, and finding out they all had different ideas was a big surprise. While it was obvious that each person had decided to make one particular component of the job his or her major focus, it was too bad for Ernest that the company only cared about having its sales goals met.

Prescription:

Executives and managers at every level have to be aware of the three components of successful performance. Those three areas are part of every leader's responsibility no matter where they are in the corporate structure. The disciplines are:

Leading: Work on creating a successful future by planning and strategizing all parts of their department or the company as a whole, especially if they are at the highest level of responsibility. This will set things in motion to grow and advance the organization. Leading requires an optimistic attitude and some willingness to risk the unknown.

Managing: This level focuses on the day-to-day and requires quick decisions and effective communication. Time spent in this area always seems to be pressing for more involvement, which can be either good or bad, depending on the situation.

Administrating: The rules and regulations that guide many organizations are Administrative in nature. In short, this area is backward looking by nature, using rules that were created some time ago to guide people when they are unsure and can't figure out new solutions. Spending too much time here can be paralyzing at times but helpful when serious challenges arise.

Ernest might not be aware of how each person sees the most important element of the job, but his performance reviews and total team meeting should spend some time clarifying how each person works in each of the three areas of Leadership.

Your Job Isn't Finished When Someone Accepts Your Job Offer

Situation:

Amir hated hearing this kind of progress update on the latest addition to join his sales team. As had happened before, the "perfect hire" had decided that the position really wasn't what she was looking for in a career opportunity. There was some mention of a position opening up at her old employer (the one she couldn't wait to leave), and the sense of familiarity there was too hard to resist. Amir really struggled with this news because the hiring process had been so well managed and the offer he made to this candidate had checked off all her boxes for a perfect job. Shouldn't this have been a real "plug and play" success story? What went wrong and how did Amir not have any idea that his new superstar-in-the-making would be leaving in just a week?

Diagnosis:

Reading between the lines of Amir's frustration and lack of awareness of what was happening indicates a couple of hiring mistakes made on his part. Amir didn't do very well in making this hire, even though in his view both he and the HR team had done a particularly good job this time. Some critical steps were missing, and some essential disciplines were lacking in order to make sure this new hire would make a successful transition to her new place of employment. Amir did just enough to get lucky once in a while but not enough to prevent these types of drop-outs when he could least afford them.

Prescription:

Amir, and every other manager who needs to hire successfully, has to carry the process all the way to completion, not just far enough to rely on a "plug and play" hiring success. The hiring procedure must include all the expected steps of good job postings, good vetting of resumes, strong interviewing methods, diligent reference and background checks, and an appropriate compensation offer. Where the process typically fails is when there isn't sufficient attention paid to asking the tough questions about why a company might not be the perfect match for the candidate, and why the perfect hire might not actually be the right fit. Also, no hiring process is complete without an explicit and highly accountable on-boarding process to assure both parties get started on a clear path to mutual satisfaction. Do not let a good hire turn into another disappointment. Put all the pieces of the puzzle in place and put them in the right order.

Must All Salespeople Follow The Same Rules?

Situation:

The situation had reached a critical point, and Margaret was still deciding what to do. Her team of nine sales people had clearly separated into three levels of performance: two were setting the world on fire and really winning, five others were on-plan and consistently above average, but the last two just couldn't seem to get out of the starting gate. As a committed manager, Margaret had created some standards and rules for the team so that everyone would know what was expected and how to succeed. As she started implementing this "ops manual," she began to realize that her top performers weren't pleased being "micro managed" like the others who were still struggling. One of the A-players was so unhappy that he used the social grapevine to send a message that he was starting to look around for a new job that would give him his freedom back, and Margaret was sure she didn't want him to leave.

Diagnosis:

Rules are essential for establishing team management consistency. A set of clearly defined standards and expectations can save a manager time and help people in all types of organizations operate profitably. Where many managers or administrators fail is when they don't realize that not all rules need to be applied to all people equally. When trying to apply a "one size fits all" philosophy to a team of different capabilities, it is not uncommon for the top performers to expect leniency with some of those rules. Their performance is better than others, so their amount of self-responsibility and self-management should match that performance level. Assuming that all team members can understand and perform to the same standards and expectations is a formula for trouble.

Prescription:

Margaret's intentions were right on target, but her implementation is what let her down. Had she established "Below Baseline," "Baseline," and "Brass Ring" levels of performance, she could determine which of her team members had to be watched closely and which ones could be left to run their business like entrepreneurs.

Demonstrate a process that shows where each person is relative to the three levels of performance mentioned above, and then create levels of accountability each person must accommodate based on how they are performing. Below Baseline people live under house arrest rules. Baseline performers get some freedom but have to report in regularly and provide documentation for their efforts. But Brass Ring players get to operate in a much less controlled arrangement with much less managerial interference. As long as they keep posting big numbers, the rules should be few and far between.

Managers can't pay equal attention to everyone, so the best managers set these standards to help them determine where their efforts can be most effective.

Final Thoughts

Did you hear, see, feel, or learn something new? Did you find even one, simple nugget you can or will use in your everyday efforts?

If so, congratulations on being open minded enough to let some new concepts inside your world. If you found more than one concept you are committed to using, then maybe you are starting to build something that really sings. That song could be a wonderful thing in the business world, where excuses, stalls, entitlement, defeatism, and unproductive behavior can start to sound deafening and irritating, like a noisy gaggle of geese. For being determined to block out that noise, go ahead and give yourself a pat on the back for the bravery to elevate your game.

On the other hand, if you found nothing you can use and thought it was all hogwash, then that's okay too. We know these ideas are not for everyone. We understand that embracing change and letting go of traditional beliefs may undermine a success formula you are already using. Sincerely, we do. So no matter what your circumstances, please be aware that we gladly welcome your feedback and would love hearing from you.

Thanks for reading this book or at least some of the stories. We hope you learned some interesting and exciting concepts that you can use to make yourself different in such a competitive environment. We see so many companies and individuals try to differentiate themselves through pushing features, benefits, pricing, or programs and forget about this one single idea: Perhaps the best way to stand out from the crowd is to get someone's attention **by the questions you ask, the way you think, how you position yourself, and the fact that your approach is not what they see or expect from everyone else.**

So we'll leave you with this last question…

If you manage, think, believe, act, and behave like a typical manager, do you have any reason NOT to be treated and feeling like so many other overworked managers?

Here's to expanding your mind and recreating your expectations for success!

Charlie Hauck

Fred Liesong

About Charlie Hauck

Drawing on more than 25 years of experience working with leaders focused on both personal and professional growth, Charlie shares his experience, creativity, and savvy in understanding his clients' particular challenges. By respecting the differences in the wide variety of businesses and industries his clients represent, Charlie believes it is the people, rather than any of their technologies, that create the most lasting successes. By making that the foundation of all his work with both individuals and teams, Charlie's clients have been successful in all types of industries and organizations, ranging from, manufacturing, distribution, non-profits, healthcare providers, and a diverse group of companies at all levels of the business world.

Past and current clients include both regional and national organizations in the professional services, distribution, manufacturing, and technology arenas. Growth Dynamics also has a wide range of experience in the utilization of instruments, assessments and processes to support hiring, as well as selection and development of individuals and teams that make up successful growing organizations.

Charlie and the Growth Dynamics team are heavily committed to bringing their expertise to many different markets where the primary focus on human interaction is immensely important to growth and success.

Charlie's pastime activities include hanging out with his grandchildren, enjoying time at the beach, skiing out West (four knee surgeries later), and riding one of his many bicycles.

About Fred Liesong

Fred joined Growth Dynamics as an associate in 2003 and became Operating Partner of the LLC (with Charlie Hauck) in 2006. He contributes the practical knowledge gained from decades of sales, sales management, and operations experience in healthcare, technology, and consulting. While he is still heavily involved with the overall operations of the company, he is also heading up the expansion of the Recruitings and Assessment practice - Growth Dynamics Talent.

A continuous and successful history of opening new territories, introducing new products, and founding his own start-up company has provided Fred with a broad perspective on the challenges of creating, growing, and retaining a solid business base. Having worked with both large corporations and smaller startup firms, Fred has acquired the skills and working knowledge needed to manage a wide variety of business issues in direct sales, channel marketing, and strategic partnerships.

As a sales professional, Fred has studied and employed many different sales and management strategies, leading to numerous performance awards throughout his career. An ability to implement any part of a growth strategy is the result of his experience in operations, mentoring sales teams, working with complex sales cycles, and analyzing opportunities in the marketplace. He is a proponent of developing repeatable internal processes that allow all team members to easily execute critical business activities with maximum impact.

Significant entrepreneurial experience came as the owner of Ultimate Software in Philadelphia, where he co-founded a VAR business focused on the highly competitive market of Human Resource and Payroll Information Systems. This eventually led to a successful IPO. During this time, he gained valuable insights on how creativity, synergistic team cooperation, and shared common goals can propel even the smallest companies to success.

Based on an ability to sense relevant strategies and tactics, Fred can provide the tools and insights to overcome the frustrations and hidden obstacles of consistently growing the top and bottom lines.

When he's not working, Fred enjoys trading equity options, riding his bicycle on the nearby Montour Trail, or fishing in his Bass Tracker on the local lakes and rivers of Western PA.

About Growth Dynamics

For more than 15 years, Growth Dynamics, LLC, has worked with businesses nationwide in search of new ideas and better results in the areas of individual and team performance. Additionally, Growth Dynamics helps companies with sourcing and selecting high caliber sales professionals and sales management executives.

Growth Dynamics provides non-traditional, counter-intuitive sales process improvement, sales management enhancement and executive development to a wide variety of businesses, including manufacturers, distributors, contractors, and manufacturers' representatives. Growth Dynamics focuses on helping people rethink many of the concepts they currently use order to shorten decision cycles, improve closing ratios, improve or protect margins and create a competitive advantage.

Past and current clients include both regional and national companies such as Pepco Sales & Marketing, Northeastern Supply, Manufacturers Marketing Inc., Brandon Associates, Preferred Sales Inc., Nexus Sales, Mullen Corp., The Granite Group, PAMS Inc., The Duff Company, Smith and Stevenson, The Granite Group, Rich-Tomkins, and Felker Brothers.

www.ingramcontent.com/pod-product-compliance
Lightning Source LLC
Chambersburg PA
CBHW070329190526
45169CB00005B/1804